MEL BAY PRESENTS

Selected Guitar Solos

VOLUME 3
by JORGE MOREL

1 2 3 4 5 6 7 8 9 0

© 2004 CHESKA MUSIC. ALL RIGHTS RESERVED. USED BY PERMISSION.
EXCLUSIVE SALES AGENT, MEL BAY PUBLICATIONS, INC., PACIFIC, MO 63069
No part of this publication may be reproduced in whole or in part, or stored in a retrieval system, or transmitted in any form
or by any means, electronic, mechanical, photocopy, recording, or otherwise, without written permission of the publisher.

Visit us on the Web at www.melbay.com — E-mail us at email@melbay.com

Table of Contents

About the Author

Now working and living in New York City, Jorge Morel began his musical journey at the age of seven in his native Argentina where his father taught him the rudiments of playing the classical guitar. He went on to study advanced guitar technique at the internationally recognized Academy of Professor Pablo Escobar in Buenos Aires and upon graduating, joined Mr. Escobar in radio and concert performances.

Morel left Argentina to perform in Ecuador, Colombia and Cuba, where he recorded his first solo LP and was featured on a weekly TV show. Vladimir Bobri, president of the New York Classical Guitar Society, lent his recognition and support to Morel after hearing him perform in Puerto Rico. This led to concert engagements in California and Hawaii and Morel's 1961 debut at Carnegie Hall. At this time, Morel recorded his second LP for Decca Records and subsequently recorded three more solo albums.

Morel's debut was followed by appearances at Lincoln Center's Alice Tully Hall and Town Hall in New York, Queen Elizabeth Hall and Wigmore Hall in London, National Hall in Dublin and Suntory Hall in Tokyo. His performances have been enthusiastically received in many countries including Argentina, Brazil, Canada, Colombia, Cuba, Ecuador, England, France, Japan, Holland, Ireland, Italy, Norway, Poland, Puerto Rico, Scotland, Spain, Sweden Finland, Greece, Singapore, Germany and the USA.

Upon moving to New York City, Morel performed nightly at The Village Gate, the jazz lover's haven-- sharing the bill with jazz legends such as Erroll Garner, Dizzy Gillespie, Stan Kenton and Herbie Mann. Around this time, Jorge met Chet Atkins and began what was to grow into a lifelong friendship. Atkins demonstrated his admiration for Morel in a very tangible way when he facilitated the recording of the artist's sixth solo album with RCA Victor. Morel was represented by Columbia Artists Management for a total of eight years during the 70's and toured throughout North American and Canada, performing approximately seventy concerts per year.

Morel continued to solidify his reputation as an outstanding artist and composer with the premiere of Suite del Sur, a concerto for guitar and orchestra which he premiered with the Los Angeles Philharmonic under the direction of Zubin Mehta. Morel continued his study of composition for a number of years with the late Rudy Schramm, a respected teacher, author, columnist, and arranger whose enthusiastic recommendation of Morel led to an appointment to a professorship at prestigious Lehman College in West Bronx, New York.

Jorge has performed internationally for thousands of audiences with a blend of brilliant technique, a uniquely personal style, and sophisticated artistic expression. In addition to his performing career, Jorge Morel has made significant contributions as a composer for the guitar, gaining the respect of his peers and establishing himself as a leader in the ongoing development of classical guitar technique and repertoire.

For more information about Jorge Morel, please see: http://www.jorgemorel.com/

to Bill Bay

Staccato Dance

Jorge Morel

7

to Wayne Bussell

Lullaby and Dance

Jorge Morel

10

11

to Tony Acosta

Brazilian Sunrise

Jorge Morel

14

to John Price

Al Guitarrero

Jorge Morel

18

20

23

Little Suite to Rebeca

Jorge Morel

28

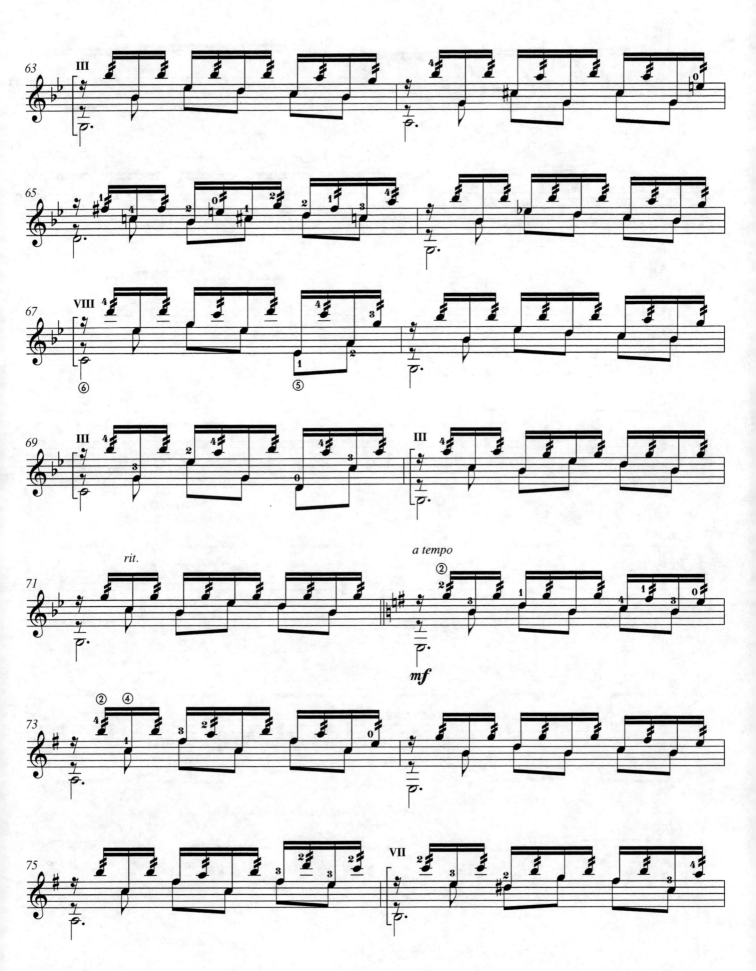

molto rit.   attacca

Allegro

32

A Mi Barrio

Pompeya

Jorge Morel

36